# AFRICAN AMERICAN'T

Ayokunle Falomo

FLOWERSONG
PRESS

FLOWERSONG
PRESS

FlowerSong Press

Copyright © 2022 by Ayokunle Falomo

ISBN: 978-1-953447-32-6

Library of Congress # 2022945436

Published by FlowerSong Press

in the United States of America.

www.flowersongpress.com

Front cover: Brittainy Moye & Ayokunle Falomo

Back cover: "[Unidentified man]" photograph, courtesy of the Library of Congress

Set in Garamond.

Typeset for FlowerSong Press by David A. Romero davidaromero.com.

Typseset design by Ayokunle Falomo.

NOTICE: SCHOOLS AND BUSINESSES

FlowerSong Press offers copies of this book at quantity discount with bulk purchase for educational, business, or sales promotional use. For information, please email the publisher at info@flowersongpress.com.

# Praise for Ayokunle Falomo

In *AFRICANAMERICAN'T*, Ayokunle Falomo deftly & tenderly tackles the nuances of African im|emigration and the subsequent journey of navigating Blackness, belonging and un|becoming in the American empire. Falomo expertly takes readers across timelines and territories, allowing us to bear witness to the consequences and contradictions of national allegiance for Black migrants in search of themselves. Yet, for the vastness of the book's subject matter, *AFRICANAMERICAN'T* is also an intimate text deeply rooted in the familial and the search of this thing called "home." This is not a manuscript to read through quickly or only once. Filled with stories, questions, lamentations & celebrations, *AFRICANAMERICAN'T* is an invaluable and generous contribution to diasporic storytelling and an invitation for writers to recognize the urgency of telling more complete stories about our origins, journeys and selves.

—Mwende "FreeQuency" Katwiwa, author of *Becoming//Black*

It is impossible to read *AFRICANAMERICAN'T* and not think of Baldwin. Ayokunle Falomo, of course, is aware of his lineage, both blood and otherwise. The poems seem to ask: how could he not be? In this stunning collection, the Nigerian, American writer explores what it means to inherit displacement; to take the country into the body; to map the distances between family, history, Blackness, life. Though Falomo states, "I never asked for America. No, I never asked for America to be mine," he has marked a place for himself somewhere in between—in Houston, among fellow Nigerians in the U.S., in between the lines of these poems he offers as familial testimony to the realities of migration. This collection is inventive, playful, curious, smart. Anyone studying language or Blackness should read it—and everyone else too.

—Ariana Brown, author of *We Are Owed.*

In *AFRICANAMERICAN'T*, Falomo tenderly traces his body on the American political map. The exciting inventiveness of language wills Diasporic histories into poetic form. This feat of a project gives those of us tussling with the many failures of nation permission to own and fully embrace a boundless grief, a righteous rage, and bountiful stillness.

—Loyce Gayo, author of *half-note thoughts*

One of the side effects of living through diasporic trauma is learning to navigate a historical-emotional past, present and future all at the same time. This paradox of Black existence is a writer's challenge... Ayokunle Falomo uses poetry to show not only how to navigate spacetime all at once, but also how to carve it into the human psyche with all its memory, weight, and breath... Falomo gives us living, breathing memories that stretch and kick and try on new clothes through such a genuine and vulnerable speaker willing to guide us through.

—*Houston Review of Books*, Aris Kian in her review of *African, American*

# Table of contents

for us;

for you, O. G.

(as record.)

*...no longer sure / which place is home / and which is more foreign...*

—MWENDE "FREEQUENCY" KATWIWA

...

*What—wonders the African—is really happening in the shadow of world events, past and present—and of world problems, old and new—to an America that seems to understand so little about its black citizens? Even so little about itself. Even so little.*

—LANGSTON HUGHES

# GENESIS

*They have a lottery. You pick people. Do you think the country is giving us their best people? No. What kind of a system is that? They come in by lottery. They give us their worst people, they put them in a bin, but in his hand, when he's picking them is, really, the worst of the worst. Congratulations, you're going to the United States. Okay. What a system—lottery system.*

—████████████████████ on Dec 15, 2017
while speaking to FBI Academy graduates

If we should at all start,
let us at birth. Let there, of course,
be a certificate of birth. Let mine,
like anyone else's, be how I prove

that I was born. It is 2018
and would you look at that,
how there is no difference
at all between the calendar

of the year I was born
and this year's, if you
pay no mind to "the dates

for Easter and other
irregular holidays based
on a lunisolar calendar."

. . .

On the day
I was born

I was born
as another would
cease to be a son
his mother can name
as alive
if perhaps
the weight of this reality
that he was born
that she birthed him
hasn't already laid
claim of her breath


. . .


And the headline says:
**WALKER BECOMES
1ST EXECUTION IN 28 YEARS**


. . .


In 1990

I was born
the first

child & son
of my mother

which means

this year
I'll be 28 &

celebrating this
will be a reminder

that indeed
I was born.

          . . .

And the news article says
he was the "first

inmate in Illinois to die
by lethal injection" & isn't

this too,
I think, a kind

of birth?

          ...

And again, the article says:
"At 12:01 a.m.,"

the buttons which the two
devoted disciples who'd been

assigned the role
of executioner pushed

delivered, to his condemned
body, the gospel, how
the end is near.

          . . .

& of course, the trinity:

one drug for him to sleep,

the second for his breathing
to stop & the third, his heart

...

& of course
before this
the last
supper:
*pan-fried*
*wild rabbit*
*gravy made*
*from the pan*
*drippings*
*biscuits*
*a dessert*
*of black*
*berry pie*
*with whip-*
*ped cream*

...

& i cannot help but think how again i'm sorry we have to start
at birth & how in order for a thing to become an answer if
hunger were to be a question it has to be first born of its mother
or of our Mother the Earth Yes let us start at birth & how if
everything must have a genesis chapter one of this would speak
of how on the 78th day from the day i was born a President's
signature like my father & mother's on my birth certificate
confirmed the birth of a thing & the thing is what will years
from now grant my father & i entry into this country where as
of today he whose name we refuse to name is still President &
the one who was then said: "Today I am pleased to sign... the
most comprehensive reform of our immigration laws in 66
years" & most days like today i still am not sure whether i am

pleased by this or not but i know if it was not birthed there would be no form for my father to sign an agreement that we were both fine with leaving who knew my mother & sister & 3 brothers behind & that we were all fine with the reality that years after i would have left i will miss them so much that i will empty my ducts until there are no more tears left in them & that my father would empty his pores or purse same thing of his hard-earned sweat up to the last drop & offer it as payment that'll grant them the opportunity to come join us but let us not speak of the years that will pass before this No No let us

*We want to be Americans, full-fledged Americans, with all the rights of other American citizens. But is that all? Do we want simply to be Americans? Once in a while through all of us there flashes some clairvoyance, some clear idea, of what America really is. We who are dark can see America in a way that white Americans cannot. And seeing our country thus, are we satisfied with its present goals and ideals?*

—W. E. B. DU BOIS

. . .

*who are you without your country*

—ARIANA BROWN

## CORPUS ALIENUM

consider        how a thing    finds its way

inside the body            a bag of nails            a boat

anchor        an ice pick    a javelin        a bicycle

pump  a drill bit        a pipe  a knife        a sword

fish    a bullet                another body & if the body

is a country    consider what        or who

is considered foreign & deemed        removable

how else to tell you this        some things

we write out the body        some things we write

the body out of

# UPON COMING ACROSS THE MIGRATORY BIRD TREATY ACT OF 1918

*For many birds, migration is instinctive, but sandhill cranes*
*have to learn to relocate. The young birds are taught*
*the finer points of migration by their parents.*
*Among the lessons learned by these birds,*
*this is a good place to spend the winter.*

## I. MIGRATORY: BIRD: TREATY: ACT:

Definition: denoting an animal
that migrates. Definition: a warm-
blooded egg-laying vertebrate
distinguished by the possession
of feathers, wings and a beak
and (typically) by being able to fly.
Definition: a formally concluded
and ratified agreement between
countries. Definition: a thing
done, a deed; a document attesting
a legal transaction:

## II. CONCEPT:

Concept:    I was born
in 1918

in Nigeria

Concept:    I was born a boy
inside a shell

I hatch & grow
into a thing with wings

Concept:     Self-Portrait as Coal as
Rapper Cold as (Shut Yo Mouf)

Because I am black as (what) but also 'cause
I'm popping & I got it going on look mama no
hands I'm fly like that look at my wings I mean
hands watch me fly allday errday & in case
uoeno hands will make her dance & if I run out
I got mo' hands hands hands I an endless supply
in the hands of my country I'm gon' party like
it's 1918!

Concept:     While taking the said portrait        of myself
as coal as rapper  the camera flashes *Get Out*
style        & suddenly I start to shed
my wings. I feel sick to my stomach & so
I vomit.                            I open
my beak wide enough to let out an entire ocean
of feathers.                     The entire room is

submerged now.        & I can't escape
                   this seemingly new thirst
for flight. Error.        Forgive me.
                   It's always     been there.

Concept:     I wake up

alive in a boy's body, a newborn
in a city I don't recognize
as mine, far away from the nest
my mother has worked so hard
to make home. I wake up

19

with my entire body painted
in white & red socks to match.

I was born
a fan of The Olde Towne Team. I
heard that yesterday, they clipped
the claws of the Chicago Cubs. We
still celebrate. Today,
                    I was born

a thing ready to be launched
inside the war-hungry mouth
of the world. Forgive me, in sin
did my mother conceive me.
It's no wonder I was born
a sin, a disease, a lesion
in the mouth of Saint-Mihiel.

Forgive me, Lord.


III. I BIRD 1918 (AN ERASURE
OF THE NIGGER STORY BIRD TWENTY ACTION 1918)

*"I remember when I was a boy—must ha' been about twenty
years ago—folks was dreadful frightened about the niggers...
'fraid the niggers was risin'.'*

— Pg. 483, AMERICAN NEGRO SLAVERY

*To keep the gunners from shattering the crop itself they were generally
given charges of powder only; but sufficient shot was issued to enable the
guards to kill enough birds for the daily consumption of the plantation."*

— Pg. 90, AMERICAN NEGRO SLAVERY

the U.S.

- is permitted        to "pursue, hunt,
  take, capture, kill,    attempt to take,
  capture or kill, possess, offer for sale,
  sell, offer to purchase, purchase, deliver
  for shipment, ship, cause to be shipped,
  deliver for transportation, transport, cause
  to be transported, carry, or cause to be
  carried by any means whatever, receive
  for shipment, transportation or carriage,
  or export, at any time, or in any manner,
  any migratory bird. . . for any part, nest,
  or egg of any such bird"
- with no        "due regard to the zones
  of temperature and to the distribution,
  abundance, economic value, breeding
  habits, and times of migratory flight"
- decree that this law is        lawful
- enforce the    seizure of birds
  illegally taken
- establish,
- enact and implement laws    to allow
  for open seasons
- repeat
- continue

  import and export
  $500                        sell
not more than $2000

        wild
  the definition of "wildlife"
under these amendments does
    not include migratory birds
and Birds in Danger of Extinction   authorize

birds and their parts illegally taken
for disposal by the Secretary of the Interior
as he deems appropriate      specify

that both nations will take      identified ecosystems
of special importance      to migratory birds

; signed.

End Note:

*Not all…bird species are protected under the act.*
*Birds that are considered non-native…are not protected,*
*and many groups… are subject to limited protection and can be hunted in*
*season.*

## PORTRAIT OF MY FATHER WITH PLINY'S BIRDS: A NATURAL HISTORY


[To THE EDITOR OF THE SPECTATOR] *SIR,* —*I am writing to ask whether any of your readers could possibly name the following small bird from my description.*


before departure: five eggs
delivered by the mouth.

*He is about the size of a small starling, wings black, with a half-inch-wide white stripe running along lengthwise down their centre. Tail also black, but edged with white. Breast is very light coloured, but not as snow white as the bars on the wings, or his head and neck, which are all very white indeed.*

highly praised
by some. rarely seen. observe,
beneath the temple, a cracked shell.
open beak. ill-omened, sacred.

*On the head he carries a white tuft, not a crest, but a regular tuft. This is about a quarter of an inch high, and gives the small bird a most fascinating and cheeky appearance.*

not fable. no one here doubts
its existence. only one

in public view. exact.
throat a crest. around

his neck, the sacred sun. head
a nest adorned with a tuft

of instructions: eat.
build. lay down. die.

*The beak is light coloured, and the eyes are peculiar, being surrounded with a light yellow circle. He is always with seven or eight of his own kind, and is a poor flyer, seldom going more than twenty to thirty yards at a time.*

head and neck thrust into the crest

and helmet of the warrior sitting on horseback.

the whole of the body, every feather

of wing and tail, concealed.

*If I can discover the bird's proper name, I shall have accomplished something. They are evidently migratory, as it is only since our rainy season commenced that they have arrived. I can detect no difference between male and female. I have not the heart to shoot a specimen, as they are extraordinarily tame, and, as I have said, most fascinating to look upon.— I am, Sir, &c.,*

# THE ONE IN WHICH MY FATHER REMINDS ME YET AGAIN OF THE GROUND, OR MY FATHER IS A PEACOCK? AN EAGLE? IDK.

*The dream of flying is as old as mankind itself. However, the concept of the airplane has only been around for two centuries. Before that time, men and women tried to navigate the air by imitating the birds.*

I was 17 when I, with my father, rode the back of a giant bird

and landed on this here soil. And here on this new soil, I plan to unearth all that I can be and lay it on the altar of my family name as offering for all the sacrifices my parents have made.

All my life, I'd been a bird who did not know about his wings & ever since I found them, all I wanted to do was soar. Excited, I asked my father once: *what are these?* And he said: *quit flapping.*

And I question myself often, if a wing is still a thing to be admired if it never works the way it was designed to. I look

out the coop and say, *daddy there's a wide and free world out there.* He says: *I flew once, you know? Let me tell you how scary it is out there.*

And I get it,

there is security here, with both feet firm on the ground. And the sky, well… who knows? My father knows safe, speaks it as fluent as his mother's tongue, and settling, for just okay or anything at all,

is a language I don't quite understand.

He reminds me too often about the ground. *Use your feet instead,*
he says. He says, *when I was your age, I walked and walked miles*
*across the village…* And I ask if this is what it means to be
grounded.

It's puzzling

how my father, this Rubik's cube of a man, could give up his
wings so I can fly yet remain unmoved when I try to. Do you
understand

how frustrating it must be to explain, *daddy, I think you must've*
*been a bird, too, or how then do you explain these wings of mine?* I, too,
am

my father's son

and although I still don't know
what kind of bird my father is,

I sure as hell
hate what flying across the ocean
has done            to his wings.

# ALIEN REGISTRATION
# (OR, THE DS-230 IS AN ANIMAL WITH 2 PARTS)

| PART I – BIOGRAPHIC DATA | | |
|---|---|---|
| **INSTRUCTIONS**: form. complete. form. copy. yourself. complete. yourself. form. yourself. mark. yourself. insufficient. answer. yourself. form. question. yourself. separate. attach. yourself. complete. form. complete. | | |
| **WARNING**: fact. false. result. exclusion. false. exclusion. fact. result. fact. result. false. conceal. fact. statement. permanent. false. | | |
| one way to identify a human is by their   her   his | | |
| name        & an Alien?        by its number      Mine: 2007AF00010225 | | |
| & I suppose since everything                 must have a name or a number<br>let's give the form a name         let's call it | | |
| an animal & if it is<br><br>(& it is) & is too capable of shape-shifting | then I | suppose I must make myself all teeth &<br>find what part of the animal<br>I can easily sink              myself into |
| maybe the neck | yes, the neck<br><br>yes, | the ink on the page is<br>black |
| but somehow                I see red<br><br>the red is my father's blood<br>this river<br>that still runs through<br>his veins  ran out<br>of his pen onto the page  & I know one day<br><br>this river of his      will      run out<br>& dry up  But I know      his mouth | | the animal is all mouth–its throat full<br>of so many pebbles         & so then,<br><br>I suppose my hands must be useful<br>for something…      if only this once<br><br>& so I will            slit open the throat<br>of the animal,        strip it of its hide<br>–<br>branded              with a 2007 – & |

| | |
|---|---|
| has already thrown up pebbles & <br><br> left them for me to find on the riverbed | pick out the pebbles   one   by one |

| | |
|---|---|
| I'll lay them out <br><br>     in no order that is <br>         particular: | 1. 1990 5. 77082 11. 1993 04 15 07 25 345 14. 15. 16. 12 |

12. 13. 30 17. 18. 06 30 1967 10

345 19. 20. 21a. 21b. 22. 23. 09

| 2. 3. 09 12 4. 5.  15 | #1904 1952 30. 345 | 2001 09 06 2001 24.25. | 16 6. 7. 8. 9. 10. 3803 |
|---|---|---|---|

## PART II – SWORN STATEMENT

| | | |
|---|---|---|
| & if I should defy INSTRUCTIONS & the <br> WARRING       & stop here      & not      complete form | **×** | No |
| it'll remind me: *I (DS-230 PART II), together with…PART I,* <br> *constitutes the complete*           *Alien* <br><br> so then,          can I claim        human <br> (or?)           I am still        alien(?) | **×** | No |

# FULL MOUTH, OPEN MOUTH

It is 2007: I walk into a country that is not: mine with a full mouth: My foreign drips down my chin from its overflow: It is 2017: and my mouth is still full: I did not trade my teeth: for a good meal: By that: I mean that even when I was: in this new country: hungry for a validation sizzling as the miracle that could only have been wrought by a mother's hands: I have walked away from the table: I mean that I know who: I am enough: to: die hungry than be fed: an identity or a name: that isn't solely mine: I am a hybrid of sorts still learning: and unlearning: what it is: that I am: I mean that I am: in awe of how holy it is to exist: in the imperfect way that I do: It is 2007: I walk into a park: into a circle of boys: the same age as I am: They are about to start a game of what they call soccer: I call it football: I say my name is [my name]: He says: *who?*

I say [my name]: He says: *yo-yo?* I say [my name]: He says: *yo man can I just call you A?* I say: A: No: You may not: B: No: you may not: B: Becoming is an unraveling: There is a gift to reward the work it takes to be: whatever creature you shapeshift into: you gloriously imperfect hybrid: B: Being called out of your name into a name that isn't even a name is a different kind of unraveling: I know it's cold outside: but be bold enough to let your brittle bones bear the burden of a body that knows what it means to survive: Wrap yourself in that coat!

C: See how easy it is for a      person to: be      an accessory in another's mouth?

It is 2010: I walk into a college campus: A friend walks beside me: Asks: *by the way, how did your English get so good? You've only been in America about 3 years: right?* And I tell him English is actually my country's official language: For 13 years: the education I received in: my own country penalized me: for allowing my mouth to: be an open and welcome floor: for my mother's tongue to dance on: So: yeah: here on this table: I have prepared for myself: a full course meal of myself: and all that I am: and still trying: to be: bones and all: My mouth is still full: but I have never stopped being hungry: And wouldn't it be a shame:

if I swallowed all my teeth          :          and let myself starve?

# ON DIASPORA: A SHORT ESSAY

I didn't know to dig deep into my own history until I heard Ariana, Loyce and Mwende talk about how deep the colonizers dug their hands into our soils.

And so, I burrow and burrow my way through the dirt and find myself at a workshop where I then throw up all the soil my mouth is full of. Not fertile enough to grow anything, but I digress. We're all sharing our experiences now; we take turns speaking of the language of the diaspora. That is, the common thread in the fabric of what displaces us. Sometimes this is by choice. Oftentimes, not.

Either way, we tear through the seams.

To be a child of the diaspora is to speak in dreams deferred and hopes shattered. It is to be stripped—skin and all. It's baring bones and being made to watch the pulverizing. We speak in crushed and groans and blood and calloused hands. We are sons and daughters of our fathers. The rough of their palms a map. It's us turning a *when I was your age*, and *remember whens* into lullabies we all know the words to. It's a hymnal we sing with conviction even when hope is a sinking ship. The sweat on our parents' faces a mighty river. We stay afloat. Somehow. It's the belief that one day, these hands will take the harvest back home to our fathers and mothers. It's harvest always on the horizon. But no hands enough for the gathering. It's some dying on the fields never to know the return to something that once was. To be African in America is to be fish, is to be fished out of water. It is to remember everything the water wishes to drown. It is to utter yourself unto dry land, but that is never as sturdy enough for your feet as you imagine it'd be. There's always something in the water that knows you by name, reaches out and begs your feet to dance your way back home. And you shuffle. And shuffle. And put one left foot in front of the other. You want to dance it right.

But home is a song your feet have forgotten the steps to.

The workshop ends. I leave for the city I now call home. I hand the man at the airport my passport and he greets me in a language that is mine. Wishes me well. And I thank him. I say: *Ese. Ese gan.* [Forgive my memory. It is possible this was from a different trip. I'm thinking maybe it's the one I took with my brother to Jonesboro, Arkansas; long ways from Houston, I know. Blame me for telling him to spread his wings & not let distance limit him. It's not easy to find a school that offers a Master's degree in Agricultural Economics, trust me. I know because I helped him with the search. Either way,] this is how to understand kinship. Through the way a stranger lets each letter of your name dance on their tongue. Honey seeping through teeth held in place by shade of gum similar to yours. Face plastered with the same smile you imagine adorned your mother's upon your arrival.

Have I told you my name and how it is a joy that fills an entire house?

I have? Forgive my memory.

# EPITAPHLAMIUM

Because, is this not love? That which demands
Our breath. Or sanity. I could be wrong,

But isn't love a kind of delusion? Let me be honest. I,
Too, often fantasize about my impending engagement

With the side of the law that marks me beautiful
Enough for the kiss of death. Because,

It's only a matter of time, is it not? And is this not
Romantic!? America on one knee. Black bodies

Always say yes. Look how Death—24 carat—looks
On us. Ain't it Gorgeous!? We share the proposal video

Across social media. The asphalt the altar for this unholy union.
Like a bouquet thrown or a garter tossed, we watch each bullet

Leave the officer's gun. And is this too not a testament
Of love!? Do you see it, how terrified I am,

A man still learning love with this one breath,
That I am next? I mean yes, I too want to fall in love

With something long enough for it to take my breath
Away but tonight, someone else's son catches the bullet.

And yes, I breathe, in relief. Forgive me this. I return
Home, alive. And yet, I wonder: am I unlovable

If a bullet hasn't yet found me worthy enough
To want to make a home of me?

Confession: I never asked for America.
No, I never asked for America to be mine.

Confession: I want to be silent most days
Until the ghost of [                    ] jogs past

The sidewalk of this glass house I have built
On sinking sand. This must be a kind of privilege.

Of course, I once thought myself safe even though
All around me are stones. By stones, I mean bullets.

# IN WHICH I ERASE [AND ADD TO THE] N-652, MY NATURALIZATION INTERVIEW RESULTS

A#: A 059 000 626

On _____ May 14 2013 _____, you were interviewed by USCIS officer [name redacted]

☑ You passed the tests

You passed wa[i]ve

[because the] US has accepted you
[based] on your ability to speak/ read/
write English

You will be tested on your knowledge of U.S. history &
[on how to] follow instructions

Written about [and for] you

You will pass for you [will you not?]

A) ☑ **Congratulations! Your application has been recommended for approval.** At this time, it appears that you have established your eligibility for naturalization. If final approval is granted, you will be notified when and where to report for the Oath Ceremony.

B) A decision cannot yet be made about your application. [This does not apply to you. Congratulations!]

**It is very important that you**

☑ Change

☑ Come

☑ Submit all

☑ Question your [self]

☑ [alien] that you are

☑ Come a copy    a copy of [yourself]

## PROPER ATTIRE SHOULD BE WORN

[For this] is a solemn and meaningful event
Please dress in respect[ability]

**NOTE**: Act [~~white~~] right
or you [will be] denied

# AN EXAMINATION OF / ON THE MONOLITH (OR, ON BEING JOYFUL & NIGERIAN)

INSTRUCTIONS:

*This is an examination in two parts. Take your time. It's okay if you are uncertain—the only thing that is being asked of you is that you respond as truthfully as you can. When ready, begin.*

PART I – MULTIPLE CHOICE:

1.   *Are you Nigerian?*

     a. Yes?
     b. Yes?
     c. Yes?
     d. Yes?
     e. No?

2.   *Do you know what it means to be Nigerian?*

     a. Yes?
     b. No.
     c. Yes.
     d. No?
     e. Maybe.

3.   *Does the Nigerian know joy or hopelessness or joy in spite of the hopelessness of his country?*

     a. Yes?
     b. Yes.
     c. Yes.
     d. Yes?
     e. All of the above.

4.    *Why should you be joyful as a Nigerian?*

      a. Why shouldn't you be?
      b. Should you be?
      c. Just be. Just be.
      d. Because… Because…
      e. Shouldn't you?

5.    *Who wants you to be joyful?*

      a. Who doesn't?
      b. Who gets to decide? Who gets to decide…
      c. …who wants what from you?
      d. And what is want?
      e. What does it mean to be or want to be joyful, or Nigerian?

## PART II – FREE RESPONSE/ESSAY:

1.    *Do you view joy as an emotion, a choice, a state*
*of being, a social construct? What does joy mean to you?*

I spent hours on a cold night with a girl once. We held hands as we walked a city that is not mine & oh what joy that was & oh what joy it was to bond over our love of words. I say who gets to decide what is a noun or a verb. Or if a thing is a thing or a place a place. I say think of the ocean—how it is a place & a thing. Or, perhaps it is a person, or an animal. & what a game we made of that. She said maybe a foundation is a person, the way a mother is & again, she said maybe joy is a person too. Oh what joy it would be, she said, to hold hands with joy & I said *here, my hands* before I told her my mother held my tiny hands once & named me the joy that fills the house. & what is a house or country if not a thing, or place, or person or perhaps an animal you can point to & say mine.

2.     *What is a monolith? Is joy a monolith? Discuss.*

I am personally of the opinion
that joy is a monolith, but decide
for yourselves. I am told a monolith
is one giant stone. And of course,
I think of my mother—a rock, solid
in the face of erosion. And if the girl
with the flower tattoo is right and joy
is a noun in the way a person is,
then joy is a mother! And do we say
a mother is no longer a giant stone
because one part of her does not
look like the other. What I'm saying is
I do not think a monolith to be a monolith
in the way we always think a thing to be.
I look through pictures of what are said to be
the 14 largest monoliths on the planet.
I find one—all 3000 ft. of black
rock. And isn't my mother, too?
Another is said to have a human
face. I decide it is my mother's.
It stands erect somewhere up north
of the capital of this country that is
my mother's. And as I remember it,
on the back of the 100 naira note
that has the face of the one with
the erect hat my mother said
my flattop reminded her of. Another
changes from blue to violet to
flaming red. And doesn't my mother,
too? And do, I because of that,
cease to call her my mother?

3.   *Imagine your mother as a country. Discuss with supporting*
     *evidence, how she is, or is not, a monolith.*

> what i'm saying is if joy is a noun
> in the way my country or mother is
>
> & anyone thinks it to be a monolith, then
> i would like to ask how many ways i can
>
> show you the face of my mother
> & we all still admire the beauty of it
>
> > every time i do even
> > though she does not always look
> >
> > like she did yesterday or 1990
> > or the year before that
> >
> > what i'm saying is a mother is a place
> > of refuge in the way Zuma Rock is
>
> & joy too is
>
> & if we name each body a country,
> let us speak of the endless wars
>
> we have won & lost
> & lost & how we stand,
>
> > still
> >
> > & isn't there
> >
> > so much joy in that?

# ALTERNATIVE

SISTER, 18: *Do you know where they got the idea for zombies from?*

BROTHER, 12: ██████████?

I.

Fact: Truth was. Truth is and will be
when all that ever was, is, and will be

ceases to be. Alternative Fact: Truth was.
Truth... will... cease to be. Alternative Fact be

an erasure of Truth. Fact, sturdy and upright as it be,
be a tree planted by the waters. It takes more than a wave

of its alternative for it to fall and find itself slanted
on the riverbank of that which we know for certain.

And it is certain that a fruit does not fall too far
from the tree that it belongs to. What I mean is

I've heard it said that Satan be the father of lies,
and Truth never birthed no alternative to claim as a son, so...

What is Truth if not that which refuses to leave its root
to be carried away with the wind! And we all have seen

it – what the wind can do! It, beast of burden that it is,
carries on its back everything; knows how to transport

to our ears a lie

from where it's made a home in the mouths
of those whose tongues find truth an unwelcome guest.

What a journey!!

II.

November 8, 2016 –

America woke up dressed in its true colors. I look at the map,
adorned by 58% white, and all I saw was red. I slept with the
blue that overwhelmed me upon realizing that 58% of America
couldn't wait for the White House to throw up, I mean throw
out all the melanin it's been stained with and instead, have the
orange puppet run his tiny hands across its walls;

I woke up to a new dawn, except there was nothing new about
the dawn. I mean that it dawned on me upon waking up that
there is nothing new about any of this. I mean that I woke up
with leaking faucets for eyes. I mean I woke up, and America
hates this. I woke up, even though in a puddle… and America
loves this, asks if it can join and take a swim.

III.

Alternative be a magician,

looks history in its face and turns it into something that isn't,
or rather makes of what isn't a thing for us all to mourn;

reminds us all to mourn in remembrance of those
whose breath the morning couldn't account for

but refuses to name their bodies;

is silent in the face of actual tragedy and when

questioned, asks: what stench? What bodies?

Instead, gives a tragedy that isn't
a name, calls it the Bowling Green Massacre
except there are no bodies in the coffin to mourn

Truth dies at the hands of an imposter and
no one shows up to mourn its demise.

Its alternative shows up to the funeral
and turns it into a celebration,

brings along thousands of people,
like those who apparently showed up to

██████████'s inauguration even though
their bodies did not come with them.

IV.

I've heard

my people say: *bi iro ba lo fun ogun odun, otito yio ba lojo kan*
Translation: a lie can travel for 20 years but one day, the truth
will find it! Translation: we need not ask or be on the long
search for

where Truth is
as long as
we still have

our voices.

## SO, HOW DOES IT FEEL TO BE A CITIZEN? OR, THE DAY AMERICA ASKED ME ABOUT MY MOTHER & I SAID: WHO? I DO NOT KNOW THAT WOMAN!*

To be a naturalized American citizen is to feast on the fattest part of the cow. It isn't the whole cow, but your plate is licked clean. You leave no bones on the plate. You chew until there is no memory left of what it was you were before this. And do you, because of this, call your mouth a traitor?

---

*shit sorry I swear shit I did
not sorry shit I did not
know I'd have to swear

off loyalty to my
mother's land. Tiny flag
in hand & a chest
full of questions, I looked
through my father's face

(like I remember doing searching my mother's
purse for something that wasn't
but which I wanted to claim as mine)

for an answer I could
not find. Only his shoulders

spoke in what I could
translate as a surrender

to fate. And the entire room of aliens
at the oath ceremony sings the anthem,

loud and proudly. I suppose to

prove their/they're ~~human~~
American. And my mouth

even now, 4 years later,
cannot sorry find shit the words
No… Wait… I think I got it now…

*O say, can you see,* ~~by the dawn~~'s ~~early light,~~
~~what so proudly we hailed at the twilight's last gleaming,~~
~~whose broad stripes and bright stars through the perilous~~
~~fight, o'er the ramparts we watched, were so gallantly~~
~~streaming? And~~ the ~~rockets'-~~*red glare,* ~~the bombs bursting in~~
~~air, gave proof through the night that our flag was still there.~~
~~O say, does that star-spangled banner yet wave o'er the land~~
*of* ~~the free and the~~ *home* ~~of the brave?~~

# FAILED SONNET

*Misery is often the parent of the most affecting touches in poetry.*
*Among the blacks is misery enough, God knows, but no poetry.*
*Love is the peculiar oestrum of the poet. Their love is ardent, but*
*it kindles the senses only, not the imagination.*

—Thomas Jefferson

Back home, a 13-year-old boy is set ablaze because he stole a
memory card from his mother's phone. First, the rope. Then
came the cane. Then, the baptism of fire. Before that, the boy:
doused in kerosene. In a picture of him, the boy—now ghost—
is no different from the boy in any picture of me as a boy:
piercing eyes, an absent smile; he wears a graduation cap and
gown, the color of which is the nation's flag—white & green.
Mother's hands fertile soil. Boy a tender plant. Of everything
that could uproot a boy from his mother's hands, who would
expect it'd be his mother's hands? Does it exist? Something I
love that will not break my heart. Or kill me. Here in America,
always there's news about a bullet claiming somebody's child.
Right now: children in chain-linked fences—no; there are
children in *cages*. Misery is no parent, God knows.

# A LAMENT FOR THE SECOND STANZA
# OF THE NIGERIAN NATIONAL ANTHEM

*Oh God of creation, direct our noble cause*
*Guide our leaders right*
*Help our youth the truth to know*
*In love and honesty to grow*
*And living just and true*
*Great lofty heights attain*
*To build a nation where peace and justice shall reign*

say it: say it is:
say true: say the just thing: say youth: say truth: say nation:
say it is true that the just thing to do is for the youth to know
the truth about its nation: say it is our right to know justice:
say oh how much we love to talk about justice: say love: say
God: say living: say right: right: say his creation build in vain:
say guide: say help: say direct: say just: say just: say just when
will our leaders get it right: say right: right: say you: say youth:
say honesty: say reign: say cannot: say attain: say grow: say
grow: say youth: say once (& again) say groan: say grew: say
grown: say stay: say no: say leave: stay: stay: say no: say brain:
say drain: say leave: say leave: say still: stay still: say no: say
heights: say attain: say no heights attained: say still: say cause:
say leaders: say cause: say youth: say you: say you: say no: say
no one: say blame: say no one knows: say no one knows the
cause: say you: say you: say you: say peace: say where: say no.
say nowhere. say it: say:

. . .

i've seen a man look fresh to death
while rocking a gold chain around his neck
in the middle of a raised platform as he,

mic in hand, is surrounded by a multitude
of people there to watch him
bring the heat & the mic is on fire

& this, of course, we call a good show

or justice, for is this not a public execution?
(well done) how it leaves us out of breath

& i have seen, too, a man
rock a flaming tire around his neck
in the middle of the street, as he,
with the item he stole in his hand,
is surrounded by a multitude
of people there to watch him
embrace the heat & the man is on fire

& this, of course, we call a good show

or justice, how we watch him slowly
lose the fresh of his breath to death

& after
what is done is done,
the multitude leave & all that is left
of the man's name is ash & bones
& the smoke continues to rise
to the skies
& there, in the clouds
is where
you, the forgotten stanza,
have made your home
& how long have you been gone,
oh forgotten one?

# SELF-PORTRAIT AS PATRIOT

*after Safia Elhillo*

mr adeniyi's geography class was my first lesson in tracing
my roots. & what is a country if not a head full of good hair
& though i do praise the hands of akinkunmi, this—the white
of wole soyinka's head & the green of the grass my mother
played in as a girl & which i pledge allegiance to—will be my new
flag: a symbol to hail my sovereign motherland, a banner without
stain to hand on to my children & their children & their children
who like eaglets will one day no longer be able to fit underneath
their wings. yes, i pledge allegiance to the eagle mounted on a wreath
for i too know how to build my nest close to the sky & don't i too soar
homeward for hours & hours without a single wing beat. oh how i pledge
allegiance to my feet, how they now dance to the rhythm of my beat in praise
of all the things that have been shield for my young and innocent heart

...

49

indeed too, i pledge to the (wh)     y-shaped rivers that run

through me. i pledge allegiance          to the red radiating sun in the center


of this flag i call body & to the costus      spectabilis—the red [sic] trumpet

that is my blood. yes, i too am      dormant in winter. & even in spring


when the sun shows her face      the bed remains the moist soil

my body is appressed to   for i too wait until the conditions are


warm enough before i start to grow    & when i do, don't i too need

as large of a space as you can make available?      i am always circling

around the edge of the pot,     always trying to escape. yes,
i pledge allegiance to     two white horses, because did i

too not inherit speed & did i not     start running shortly
after i was born a colt?     (mother said i did not crawl)

    & here i am, 17.5 hands of a stallion & still running
i pledge allegiance to speed,  each bone of my hands an ode

to bobsled & skeleton—the gods     of velocity the bodies of adeagbo,
onwumere, omeoga & adigun     became altars for. oh, how i pledge

to the wind these mares     leave behind when they move
& oh, how this moves me & my pen     moves in worship

...

oh god of our bodies     help us build ourselves

    into a nation     where oppression is

no anthem. & where my pledge     of allegiance is to hands


that of my daughter & sister & that of my brothers & father

& mother & that of those who mothered & fathered

    them & yours & mine & yours—each line


on our palms a river flowing into another & another & another

yes, indeed i pledge to this country of hands, the only country

faithful i know & which i wish to serve & defend & uphold

## POEM IN WHICH I AM WRAPPED IN THOUGHT & SO, WRAP MYSELF IN MY COUNTRY'S FLAG

GREEN

i'm on YouTube, listening to a song for
toddlers about the color / green. someone comments
that they are color // blind and came here to find
out what green sounds like. / now imagine a world
where no one sees color, // green specifically.
anyways, two people agree on this: / green is not a
creative color. // president buhari might agree. i am
not here to convince you / otherwise but if you want
to know how creative a color // can be, ask me what
i know about Youth and I'll speak / of the forest and
leaf after leaf—each with color // likely to be
drained from their veins, if no one hears /
them—falling to the ground. what color, // dear
listener, would you imagine hope/for a decaying
country to be? i say the color // green. & i can see
how easy it is to mistake a boy / for a tree stump, but
ask kareem about the color // of possibilities, in
spite of the bleak we know / of unavailable resources
and opportunities. color // me jaded, like the rest of
the country and you'll be right. / today, i listen to the
10-year-old boy talk about the color- // ful future
he's imagined for himself, one where his art / finds
its way into a museum, a permanent color // on the
fabric of history. i listen to the boy tell me / how he
sees himself, color- // ed as he is, no limitation,
among the great artists in the world / and the future
steps out, dressed in green—her favorite color.

WHITE

i almost left this space

blank, intentionally… but i do not
have that kind of privilege, how You do not
see color; to say, for example, the flag

of my country of birth is,
well, just a flag; ignore my knuckles,
they are just knuckles; no one cares
what color they are; there are many
ways to write and rewrite history.

i know; so let this space
be a monument / an ever-present
reminder / a catalog of failures
i imagined me reimagining

each song on the **white** album's track list
but wouldn't it be too obvious, like a red
stain on a white cloth, if i say, for instance,
"track 2, side two" of having to remind
You of such hits like slavery, genocide,
colonization… how does that sound?

it's been a "track 7, side three"
time coming & i want to talk
about revolution, but can You
tell me what happened
to all the other revolutions
between "track 1, side four"
and "track 5, side four?"

i'm not sure
exactly what
i'm trying
to tell You,

but this is where my research has brought
me: "Cyphochilus is a genus of beetles
with unusually bright **white** scales
that cover the whole exoskeleton."

i would say do what You will
with that information but that's too
easy a metaphor for inculpability.

i mean to say You can find
every visible color in the color
**white** You might not
believe me. imagine
an all **white** jury.
if You will, if You will,
grant me the permission

to invoke an expert.
enter Dr. Vignolini:
picture a red wall, a girl
wishing to be a shade or two
lighter than the one she woke
up with. do I need to tell You
what the color of the girl is?

well, have You ever weaved
a basket? imagine her hair,
each strand a palm frond.

question: how do You
make the red wall

disappear? clap

on it layers and layers

white paint. another hue

this is the beetle produce
white scales? it is flecks

all other colors. i didn't
come up with this. argue
with science. i dare. You

GREEN

the sun is still shining & my country is
all chlorophyll. i want this to be the whole
truth. i want to think of all the oxygen
left in us. how easy it is to breathe
when you think of everything that will
sprout again. everything in your dream
is green. even the grass is. tattoo this
on your forehead. remind yourself
of the legend of the boy and the green
snake. think of the boy and everything
that still isn't dead. yes. including   you
& you & you & you & you & you & you

# PRAYER

*for Erica Garner & Breonna Taylor &*
*Oluwatoyin Salau & the Chibok girls & & &*

what in this country Lord this country of soot
where breath is easily snuffed out of a body
Lord what is this country this country that

is not my father's Lord what in this country
can a father promise his daughter but smoke
Lord my sister Ebony says no one turns over

the earth when a black girl goes missing Lord
when a black girl goes she goes like smoke and
no one turns when a black girl goes when she

goes missing Lord she goes and Lord I've been
and not been no one Lord I have no tools with
which to turn the earth except my pen which is

a useless shovel Lord the bed I rest my body
on is asphalt Lord and in my sleep I turn and
back in my mother's country there is a chorus

of mothers still singing to no one bring back our
girls goes the refrain of the song bring back our
girls they sing they sing bring back our girls and

I being no one join the chorus and I sing and sing
bring back our girls with the wings on their backs
intact with words I string them back to the backs

their mothers backed them with I sing them back

into their mother's arms I sing them wings I sing
them and sing them back and Lord I bring them

# LORD        TEACH MY THROAT

to be a whale

I know my voice is
Jonah / It too is bent
on doing its own will
most days but    oh

Lord   teach my throat
to swallow my voice whole
Let there be   oh

Lord   not even
a sequestrum or even
the tiniest piece of
my tongue
left
to speak of the years
of silence that ran
like   r    i    v    e    r    s
through two continents
& how
on the phone

Mother asks: how are you?
I say: fine / I ask: how are
you? / She says: fine / She
says: I hope it is not
too cold over there
& you're staying
warm / I say: yes
/ I ask: how are
things in Nig-
eria? / She say

s: we thank
God / She s
ays: it still
is how it
was like
when y
ou left
with y
our d
ad /T
hen:

## MY MOTHER SAYS I SPEAK IN MY MOTHER TONGUE

with a tongue she does not recognize as hers,
says i sound like a foreigner & i am. my tongue is

a foreign thing in this country
i call mouth. i question myself

if it will ever be a thing my mother can be proud
of like she is her son. & she is, that much i know

but i cannot stop questioning myself.

Q: *Pin awon oro ayalo wonyi*

... *(ii) Bibeli*    *(iii) Peteru...*

...*(v) Paradise...*
... *(xiv) Pensu*    *(xv) Tabili*

   *sin abe isori afetiya ati afojuya*

A: of course, this is about language
& who

& what the language holds
   in place

& also, how the tongue holds
   back from fully expressing itself
   in the company of others
   because of shame

& or fear

of being judged

& of course, i have not forgotten
  about the questioning

& too, the question

& how it wants me
  to categorize the given loan words
  into different types: one type borrowed from
  how we hear the words pronounced

& the other from
  how we see them written

& of course,
  i think of God
& the Bible
& how i am a lone word in the mouth of God
& i think of paradise, a reward for a job well done
& i think of the work it takes to be
& i think of how i have thought my tongue to be
  the Messiah
& of course, i think of Peter
& how i too have denied my tongue
  again
& again
& again
& how, if you look closely at the roof
  of my mouth, the rooster is still crowing
& how i am a pencil – breakable, yes
  but also, in the hand of God, indelible
& how every morning i'm alive
  is the coaster on the table which holds
  the fresh cup of coffee my breath is
& how because of this i have not yet

spilled or slipped or shattered
& how my tongue isn't
   too sure of itself

but still, i begin
   again
& again
& again

until my tongue is my )question( tongue
is )stop( my tongue is my )stop( tongue
)question( is my tongue )stop( is my tongue
)question( is )stop( my tongue
is )question( my tongue )stop( is a tongue

my mother can welcome inside
the place of refuge
her mouth is, a tongue
she can look at

& say: *my son! )omo mi(*
  *you've been out in the sun*
  *working. well done. )kare(*
  *i am so proud. welcome*
  *home, son. )kaabo( welcome*

  *home. how was the journey?*

# FOR SAMUEL AJAYI CROWTHER

At 12, you were captured      along with the rest of your kin

    Reminds me of      my youngest brother who, newly

12, swears this means      he is now a man. I think of him, two

    Years before, walking into      a country that is not his. Assimilation

A white cloth, his mouth      wiped clean of my mother's

    Tongue. I speak in Yoruba      to my brother and he responds

In English. I have always wondered      how your name (especially

    Your last) isn't like mine, Crowther      even though they taught us that

You spoke in the same tongue      I thought once to buy a shovel for

    Yes, in this new country, I wanted to      dig a hole deep enough to

Engulf home. But I still have this name—traceable. My American

    Doesn't know how to walk into      Anywhere without leaving

A trail of blood that'll lead Everyone to where     I tried to bury

My Nigerian. I am Nigerian     but not in the way my father is

   My youngest brother is too     but not in the way I am. I am

A man too but I do not think I am     like my father is. Did you,

   Like my brother, think yourself a man at 12?     When your mother

A descendant of an actual king,     birthed you, did she

   Ever fear the day     your body would mistake a slave-ship

For a throne? Ajayi, shall I call you     by this, this name that belongs

   Also to my father's father or by the English     name my father, Joshua

And my mother, Ruth     did not bless me with? Did you

   Know this name of yours means born     face-down? Did you

Assume the posture of supplication     from the womb? Samuel,

This name of yours means God has heard.      And wasn't it fitting

That you'd be a gong?      That you'd wring their holy book

Into this language      they couldn't scrub clean

From your tongue? Even if  the whole mouth

Swallows an entire      tongue, the aftertaste of loss still lingers

Crowther, did you know your name      was derived from a stringed

Instrument that is now      archaic? But here you are, —

Echo loud and in tune      with the heartbeat

Of a boy you do not know      by name

And who is, too,      though under different circumstances, far

Away from home—      even more than a century

After a stroke stole the last note      from your throat

## MY BROTHER, [          ]


     If the heart to heart
Conversations I have, of recent,
Been having with my brother [        ]
Are any indication, I'll be, one day,
A good father. Unquestionably,
       I am terrified

Of fatherhood. If America allows
       Him this, he will one day be
A father too. Parapraxis: I'm sorry,
I said [        ]. Actually, his name
       Is Peace. Ironic. Lately, he's been
All trouble. There's been so much

Trouble with his behavior. My father's
Talks with him. Mine. My mother's.
       Whoopings even. All ineffective.
Nothing changes. And verily, this
       Is a bulletproof way for a black boy to
Toy with his future, you know? After all,

There is such a promise as school-to-prison
Pipeline. Sounds almost made up. Kinda
       Like the Loch Ness, this beast that's all
       Stomach. Don't even ask… It makes
A memory of the bodies of brown and black
Boys especially. Yes, I've even made him

       Write summaries of what
He understands about being
Swallowed whole by a rip, because
       It is never too early to let a black boy
Know the future America has mapped

Out for him. Dead or alive, a sentence

      Is a sentence. Before this happens,
The solution my parents are proposing is to
Send him back home. At least back home,
The whole village can raise him. At least
Back home, it's easy to tell the son of whom
      He is. At least back home,

The boy won't be called out of his
Name; won't be given a name
      That doesn't belong to him.
      I hope I never stop talking to him
About life. Our hands too, how with them
We choose what we mold or break. Because,

Here in America, 12 years isn't
Too young for a black boy
      To be named ghost.

## S.M., THE YOUNG AFRICAN PAINTER RESPONDS

dear phillis
i'm sorry that it's taken me centuries to get
back to you i hope it's not too late i'm sorry
too that i am not responding to you
in my own voice phillis i have borrowed
the mouth of a young african
poet who claims he does not always know
what to say although he does say an awful lot
for someone who doesn't know what to say
in any case i have a lot to tell you phillis
i who was given a name by the one i was given
to who received me like property passed down
from a gracious & thoughtful father to his son
phillis the one i belong to was given by his
father the name john which means YAH
WEH is gracious & isn't he his *splendid city*
*crown'd with endless day* if ever we will meet
i cannot wait for the day when we will have no need
for words or paintings but until then these words
phillis the name you were given it means loving &
here's something you might or might not know we
share the father of the one you were given to gave
him the same name as the father of the one
i belong to & phillis was he in any way like his
father no need to answer that let's pray instead
that we become everything our fathers & mothers
couldn't be you be a green bough that remains
fastened to the trunk & i will be a branch from
a tree with thick or callused skin which bears
semblance to a scepter & if you be a meadow
of wheat phillis then a land open & uncultivated
i'll be & what bliss how everything that finds root
here in us *blooms in endless spring* yours
                                    scipio moorhead

69

## SORRY I AM NOT HIM I AM THE OTHER AFRICAN POET

*for Yaw*

it's not that it's all that remarkable
but twice this week I have been

asked if anyone has ever told me
I look like donald glover & I suppose

I do next time I will pretend I don't know
who he is & say no one has ever told me

I look like danny glover but thanks

I guess & perhaps they'll say something
about childish gambino & *this is america*

& still I'll claim ignorance & afterwards
I will erupt in laughter but before then

let this one be about blood & how
much of it was shed to make us

brothers yes we are & were
long before the colonizers came

to invade our mother's womb

## PALINODE

The bird in my hand?

I cannot always tell if it's

a raven or a crow...

Forgive me.

[          ] remains

dead. My youngest brother is

no longer 12.

# XENOMORPH XX121

*for Bolaji Badejo*

Brother, though you are not exactly my brother
in the way Deji, Tobi and Peace are, you are
my brother still. If only for the sake of blood:
how easily its cells break down.
                              The body a country
inherited. In your case, you know exactly which
parent to blame: both. My body always aching,
some days I do not feel at home in my body. I
wonder if you ever felt this too. How did it feel
to be in an Alien suit? Tall as you were. Brother,
I must've been seven, or eight, when I first became
aware of my blood. G6PD deficiency is what
the doctors called it. I peed, and my pee was
the color of Coca-Cola. That was then. Of the blood,
there are types and there are groups. Simple
biology. It's one of the first things we're taught.
I don't remember exactly which building it was
I first learned this but I remember the disease
that claimed your breath came, too, for Sister
Gerald's secretary's. I'd call her sister, but she is
not. Not in the way Gloria is. But really, what's
a tribe? Of the blood: antigen & Rh factor. And,
too, though it has more to do with language and less
with blood, the *h factor*: how generous we are, some-
times, the tribe we belong to, brother, with words
that begin with a vowel. Hit happens by hac-
cident. For hexample: how hay man might find
han happle's core lodged hinside his throat.
Perhaps it is by accident too, how the hemo-
globin—stiff rod—turns the supposed-to-be
disc-shaped red blood cells into a sickle.

## HOW CAN I GIVE A NAME TO WHAT I AM

still searching for? Which I, perchance,
might find this sunny afternoon in May.

I'll get to it. A man is dead. Today,

across the country, people run or walk
2.23 miles to celebrate his birth.

I said, [          ] is *dead*. I meant
to say that he was killed. Something

about legacy: a father, a son. O ailing
country, the blisters

on your heels—how long before they heal?

[          ], the day I heard that you were
killed, I did not watch the video. I chose

to masturbate instead. I wish I did it
as a revolutionary act

but no. I was tired and desired
pleasure for myself. Today, I cannot

run and so I'm walking. The birds are
chittering—are these poems?— I don't know

what the fuck about. And now, thanks to
the wind, these three poles with no flags

in front of the E.C. Northern Memorial
Scout Service Center make their presence

known, as if to say, *We're here,*
*motherfucker.* I think it's laughable

to think their clanging
is a poem too. But still, I think it.

Fuck Heidegger. And poems, too—
what are they useful for? What good

is a poem if it can't stop a bullet? I'm
tired. I'm tired of thinking, of thinking

everything is a poem. I'm tired of
repeating myself like a man

singing the blues. Nothing that hasn't been said
already. There's nothing new

under this unforgiving sky, about this poem...

But O, if I must die, America, let it not be
by the hands of your unwholesome sons.

Men who take

the law into their own hands. Who,
with their hands, know nothing else to fashion
out of a body besides its ghost. Let them

keep their soiled hands away from me.

But O, if they kill me, please let them
kill my mother too. Let her not live

to mourn her son. This poem—

let it be a hex I place on everyone

who watches the video of my murder. Whoever
shares it, I pray for withered hands. Wherever it might

be shared—on WhatsApp, Facebook, You-
Tube, Twitter, or Instagram—let the apps
crash. I pray a virus on each device.

I know that I must die and will not die
on any day that does not rhyme with clay.

I know that Vallejo died on a rainy Friday
in Paris and Justice did not

die in Miami so if I must die, if I must die
in this strange land, if I must underneath

your wretched sky, America,
let it be in Houston. Let it be on a winter

day a foreigner might mistake for
summer. Let me die next to the taco

truck outside the yellow house
on Westheimer. Let me die

as black as Rothko's paintings.
As loud as the resounding quiet
of the Rothko chapel. Let me die

taking my sweet, sweet time just like
the near decade-long construction
on 290. Let me die a death that will

slow you down, America, a death like

the traffic on 610 during rush hour.

Let my body take ten thousand years
and a day to rot. And when it does, let it

not smell. Let it be so heavy, my body,
my dead body, let it be so heavy it'd be
impossible to move from where I die.

If I must die here, if my body cannot be,
will not be, returned home,

whole, if I must be buried here
on stolen land, if my body in death
must eventually fertilize this land where

nothing dies that does not
make something else flower,

my ghost will forever roam

the Surrealism room at the Menil,
where I have walked

hand in hand
with every woman I have ever loved.

I am returning from my walk
now. The brightness of the day is

giving way to a darkness accompanied
by rain. I'll be honest. I can't say why

I walked; I know it will not bring you

back, [            ]. Just like this poem.

And still, I keep on

writing it. Though I do not yet have
the name for it, I know

it can't be justice: what I want.

## FUCK THE POLICE IN AMERICA NIGERIA EVERYWHERE

*My entire Oeuvre is against the police*
*If I write a Love poem it's against the police*

— Miguel James, trans. Guillermo Parra

If not for desire, which stokes its
embers, I wouldn't know

to understand rage, its clarity, but
needless to say, I object. To *fuck* the police,

I mean. If you do, I worry about your sanity.
I question whether or not you love yourself.

*Blue balls for the men in blue. I like that.* The man
at the protest march tells me, after I say no

to us fucking the police. We laughed.
And so, let's say I meant it

as a joke, although it is no joke: the work
of trying each day to kill (not kiss!) the cop

inside my head. Less so the implied violence
but more to do with the desire

to deny pleasure is what my objection
is all about. To extinguish the possibility

of The Law misinterpreting *fuck you* as a
come-on. O, how English exhausts me.

# MAMA SAY

back when she first got here way back when she didn't
know no better long before she seen *When They See Us*
or *how* they see us if they do at all before she
understood her son's foreign tongue was no shield or
weapon he could wield my mama say she scared say
she seen the way I talk to whiteAmerica & she real
concerned that I'ma end up starving if I keep biting
the hand that's feeding me say how whiteAmerica not
gon' slap the spoon outta my mouth take the plate
away from in front of me & smash the whole table
mama say [my name] be careful say remember you a
foreigner the people you say you 'fighting for' don't
even be fighting for theyselves like that so I say well
I'm a black man in America so I really be fighting for
myself too mama & she say why whiteAmerica I say
who else I shoulda said I'm fighting 'cause every time
I step out of the house my return ain't guaranteed & I
wanna return don't you want that mama I seen the way
your face light up every time I return no matter how
long I been away from home it's like the day I was
born all over again

## SOME DAYS I STAND IN FRONT OF THE MIRROR AND REMIND MYSELF

that I am black. I could lie to you and say I'm not guilty of this, but some days, I ask my reflection—besides the obvious, which is repetition—the difference between black and 'black black' even though a bullet doesn't care about semantics. & really, what does a bullet care about besides its need to satisfy its hunger? & did you know I didn't know I was black before I crossed the Atlantic? I'm sorry. I take that black back. When I said crossed, I meant flew over. It is not exactly the same thing, but it is. Though I am ashamed of history, I'm even more ashamed to tell you this: I don't know how to swim, even if it is what will save me. I see a picture of Wade in the water—chest bare, arms raised, in spite of the history of shame—and think: Who alive in this body, in this country, has not inherited shame?

## IN WHICH I INTERVIEW MYSELF AFTER WATCHING BLACK PANTHER

*So, I'll just go straight into it. First question: What, to you, does it mean to be African?*

Well, to borrow from Ryan Coogler, I'll say it is a thread—weft or warp—running through & across the Earth, this fabric we know by no other name but Mother. I mean, I mean that we wear it on our skin, proud & loud. It is the music that moves me & at the same time keeps me rooted in spite of everything that's tried to displace my voice.

It is nothing I can escape, for my face, this metal alloy, like that of those sculpted & unearthed, long before she was, from the soil where my mother was once a girl—the land they say Oduduwa turned cradle for my people after his older brother, drunk off palm wine, could not fulfill the order of Olodumare—or my tongue, still heavy of home & traceable, will always give me away like my fathers & brothers once did theirs & their mothers & sisters too in exchange for nothing of worth.

*That's heavy. A crown of thorns of sorts—bleeding scalps and all. For what it's worth, it's quite painful to come to terms with that aspect of our history as West Africans and for those of us who weren't enslaved, our complicity.*

Yes, indeed. On the movie's release day, I, face-down on his table, as his fingers relieved me of pain, asked my massage therapist Kris, who is American in the way that I am not & African, but not in the way that I am, if he had seen the movie. He said yes & I hadn't yet & we couldn't say much about it since he wasn't one to spoil, but still we talked of displacement & how beautiful it is to belong somewhere & know that you do, even if you haven't been there before. He said he thinks he might be from West Africa.

And I said, very well you might since most enslaved Africans were/are. And he said he would, one day, love to return home & then told me how lucky I am to know the tribe that claims me as son. And I said yes, & please go, Mother is waiting with open arms to once again wrap around her sons & daughters who were once ripped from her bosom.

*Next question: So, my friend Ryan (not Coogler) says you're the real-life M'Baku. Another friend, Konji, says you remind her of T"Challa. What do you say to that?*

I say, what are friends if not mirrors! They reflect you back to you. Ok. Ok. I say, I see myself because they would not turn from the truth of all I am or let me turn away from the stare down (always) between who I am & think myself to be. And I am eternally obsessed with mirrors. Hence, I'm always speaking in self-portraits. I stand with shoulders slouched before them & I am reminded to stand up straight & pick joy up like the weapon I've known it to be even when I do not want to be reminded of this & would rather wallow in my sad.

But I am reminded how much of a warrior I am. I too am always trying to return the future to a past I don't seem to know how to let go of. I too feel the strain on both shoulders, how heavy they are, most days, with the weight of my entire tribe & the stories that bleed out of me that no one else would tell if I do not. Oh how the truth I speak has been a burden too, for there have been ears who, when they are made to listen, shrink like the *mimosa pudica* I touched as a child & which my kin from a tribe not mine call *kpakochuku* & which the hands of *Nwaoga* touched & he couldn't but see its potential to generate electricity that could, possibly, light up an entire household or country & oh, how I praise his tenacity, how he is not intimidated by this gorilla-sized dream. Yes, I too have been told of my potential to generate that which would make another feel intimidated, though I do not wish this to be true & even though my frame is nothing like M'Baku's.

*Yes! So much yes! Would you say. . . Sorry, uh, I didn't mean to cut you off. . .*

It's ok. *Are you done?*

*Yeah, sorry. Please continue.*

Ok. I mean. . . I mean, seriously, it's fine. Are you done?

*Yeah. Please go on.*

Ok. I'll leave you with this: I am my father's son, surely, & I have stared at a mirror long enough to be tempted to mistake his mistakes as a dictionary. But I say no, don't scare me like that, colonizer. I define myself. I name each new day I wake up to Challenge Day. And the truth is I do not want to be king, just a man, a good one. And most days, my father is a good man even though there is a lot he did not prepare me for, but I will not name this a failure. *WOOF* No & this will not be a feast I feed my children. Thank you.

*Thank YOU!*

# NOTHING GHAZAL

*Blessed are the meek for they will inherit nothing,*
*a nothing so big they will pray to it.*

—Loyce Gayo

Son of man, did I not tell you say you be king over
everything? / So tell me why you still dey chop shit
when nothing // dey here for this garden wey no fit
grow if you water am. My people / follow Imam go
for Mecca, follow Pope go for Rome. & still, nothing.
// Them say, In *Spiritum Heavinus*. Say, *Allahu Akbar*.
Them / forget the long long time when Englishman
arrive with nothing // in his hands but left with so
much more than he came with & if / you shine your
eyes you fit see how much he left us with—nothing.
// Them no wan remember say we tried to fight back
but he armed / some & ordered them to kill their
brothers who had nothing // to fight back with. He
said: beat dem and kill dem or if not / that, beat into
them that di black man is nothing // compared to the
Englishman, and is inferior. Said: Englishman / is
good. & England is di best place on earth, there's
nothing // bad in it at all. Because, did the LORD not
look at everything / he had made and call it good?
Tell them America is nothing // but di best place too,
he said. Say it's practically heaven. / Don't say it is
only to those who think they have nothing.

# ODE TO THE OTHER N-WORD

*after Danez Smith after Rj Wright*

how many times i've practiced
how best to fold my tongue for you
though before this, i did not sing along,
stayed quiet when the chorus of the rap

songs were nothing but *nigga nigga nigga*
and ain't the chorus always. o niggas
i can't or don't say nigga in front of,
this too is for you. you Michael

Jackson/Blackson black. neega, the first
time a nigga called me a nigga, he meant
well. meant brother. then, i thought
you more twine around the neck than

vine in vineyard & by that i mean
history serves blood thinned with
water in a glass & my niggas toast,
red wine in hand, to you & it was

hard at first to tell the difference.
nigga, you equal part comfort and
discomfort. you step into a room and
staff of moses the sea of people in it

into a quiet so clear like the dryland
them niggas walked through to get
to the 'promised land' or the room responds
in a chorus like the roaring sea, mouths

dripping with all that milk and honey
and all my niggas don't worry whether
they can swim or not but dive straight
in and drown in it. nigga, my nigga

rj say *you can't say nigga if you not black*
& my niggas argue, still, about whether
or not they have the right to allow you
citizenship in the mouth of their niggas

who are not niggas. nigga, you disrespect-
ful as hell. all dante's nine circles of it.
how you say: *no, conqueror of tongues,*
*you can't have this one. every other world,*

*word, is yours.* & nigga, you ours. even
when we don't all claim you, you still.

## A TRANSCRIPT OF AN OVERHEARD CONVERSATION BETWEEN MARGARET WALKER AND YOUNG THUG

*for my people*

: Jeffery,

at what age did you discover you were black
& small & different? Have you always been?

When you were but a child,

did you ever mistake your teacher's arm
for a mirror? Did you ever see yourself

as broken? The Fader say you sound

like a broken wind instrument, Jeffery.
I hear you say you don't know how to sing

& maybe that is true. But if you'll let me, let me

honor the years that honor how we try to be
anything at all. How once, you told us

how you came from nothing & then reminded

us again & again. Once, too, a poet spoke
of the god of trying & oh how I am a disciple.

May I praise it, then, that you are no disciple

of convention? How you try to fashion

87

for yourself a world where there is no

Adam or Eve? How in your world,

a gangsta can choose to wear a dress
or baggy pants? This (& more) you have done

for your people, Jeffery. May we all know
what it means to be this free.

: First of all, aye lil' boo.
                          What do you hear when
you hear me say I'm gon' have a shootout
& call it a parade?
                          Of course, we gon' take lives.
I'm ready to die but we never die, this you already
know. We multiply. What's death? What's breath
lost? What's another mother crying over another son
who won't return
                          home with his breath? Though too grown
for lullaby, tonight, his mother wishes once more to sing
him a song before he is rocked to an eternal sleep.
          It's war out here, I do not need to tell you
this. & to the untrained ear, our martial songs
          sound just like dirges. But we don't cry
          for our dead. Instead, we pour one
out for the bodies bullets continue to mistake for
          bottles. I mean, look at all that blood pouring
          out of them. & over here, we just call that
another day. I woke up. How's that for a miracle?
Last night I prayed, thankful for this. & every day
I pray a nigga don't test me
                          to the point where I'm tempted
to spray. I be trying, I promise. Me and my niggas be
trying to stay above all this shit, you know. We eagles
& we gon' keep flying high. Well, until fuck niggas try

bring us down to they level.

: You know

much about eagles, Jeffery? You know
they're apex predators?

: What's that mean?

: They are on top of the food chain.

: Word. I guess
                if me & my niggas
are eagles, then we eating. & trust
me when I say we put in work.
Every day, we in the kitchen,
cooking. Just like my flow is, it's hot
out here in these streets
                like a motherfucking skillet.

: You know

there is an eagle, red,
on the coat of arms of Nigeria?

: Oh word? Damn. I ain't
  even know that when

I made the song.

# AFRICANAMERICAN'T SONNET

*to be read from bottom to top*

& still I am American. But please refrain from asking
what I think about America. I know *you* expect me
to say *love*. *Once*, I belonged to one country. & now,

between my father's bedroom & my mother's, there
is a border I have to cross to get to the fridge. I don't
know which country to claim… Which country does

it belong to? I ask. This loaf of bread, this jar of milk.
I have been here for more than 10 years & I have not
returned home. Please don't ask me if I miss Nigeria.

I don't. I know you expect me to think it a betrayal.
My mouth a sheath, love & betrayal both are swords.
Perhaps it is true what the poet said of love: how

it means breathing in two countries. Is it betrayal
then? That I am here. Still breathing, even if barely.

# IT'S TRUE. I LEFT A *SHITHOLE COUNTRY*

for another one. How sad, how hard it is, to uproot
one's life and then, to plant one's family in a country
that can't keep them alive. Of course, I know no country
can. Listen. I'd love to tell you about the day I left home
except I don't remember much of it. Not what I wore. Not
what my father wore. Not how I got here. No. I drank from
the river Lethe and found myself awake in a strange land.
But, I do remember this: somewhere between Sky and Earth,
I lost my passport. I got here in November. On a day
like any day a bird leaves its mother's nest. Few days after,
families would gather across the country to give thanks
for whatever they had to give thanks for. Each year,
on the anniversary of our arrival, I like to thank my father
for bringing me here but some years I can't remember
the exact date. Was it the 25th or the 27th? Yes, it was
cold. I don't remember if I had a coat. Years later, we'll
gather around a small table that can't fit us all but still
we make room for laughter. Reunion is a cruel name
for how we meet again the hurt that can't be brought
to heel. The truth? I am a poet because my memory
is shit. What else am I supposed to write about except
what hurled me into poetry the way Ireland hurt Yeats
into it. Somewhere I read that if you look close enough,
a map can be a mirror. And so, I mirrored the topography
of my hurt and all I saw was my own face. Each poem
a bridge to a past that no longer exists. O memory.
You untamable thing. Impossible horse. My mother,
too, is thrilled by you. How you bring back to me,
in the middle of the kitchen of the house my folks now
call home, the things we thought drowned in the ocean
we know Time to be. I remember the white of my father's
uniform and how my classmates mistook him for a doctor.
I remember how I did not buy a lab coat for science class

but instead wore his uniform. And too, the many experiments
conducted on bugs whose wings I clipped. A psychiatric nurse
back home, my father became a correctional officer; traded his
white uniform for a grey one and that's the American Dream.
To say *abolish prisons* would mean I want my father hungry
and his home foreclosed. And yet, I say it. I remember, too,
the last meal I had in my country before the then-near-future
readied itself to whisk me away although I don't remember
what the face of my mother looked like when, or before, I left.

## I WALK INTO EVERY ROOM AND DO NOT NEED TO YELL WHERE THE NIGERIANS AT

*after Jose Olivarez*

because we're here: everywhere.
      loud. & colorful. & yes

      we know crooked but o bless
our mothers' hands. what miracles

they carve out of our spines.
      what blessing it is to swim

      in the rivers inside our fathers'
and mothers' palms. & how we toil

to prove that the way
      they move with the wind or

      the current of the sea is not
in vain. it's why we're everywhere:

in & on the courts, in hospitals, on tv, on
the radio, in books. to make, especially,

our father's smile. each smile a snow
      leopard we've seen maybe once

      or twice. can't remember where
but we sure do remember the holy of it.

      we're here, singing our songs
and dancing our dances, laughing

with gravity—a long
      lost kin—as it gently rocks

      a paper note after another
from sweaty foreheads to the ground.

# THRILLER NIGHT

*for James & Charles*

Crossing Westheimer, the three
of us, just before it becomes Elgin, we
head towards the yellow house where,
before this, poets had gathered but
now, two cop cars with beaming lights
are parked in the parking lot. We lean
against my car and laugh, as if we
weren't frogs inches away from a night
adder. Perhaps naive to think it but
we had no reason to believe we were
in danger, or that we were dangerous,
and so, we laughed with our whole
bodies, their lights still on us. Steady
as a surgeon's hands. We would have
left but could not leave; no one could
with the cop cars blocking the gate.
And so, we continued, the three of us,
as night became more night. Just like
a boy looking into a mirror might see
his father's face where his own face
was only minutes prior. Eventually,
they step out of their cars and walk
towards us. Something we cannot hear
is muttered into the walkie-talkie...
I'll keep it short. There was a break-in.
Cops were called. We fit the description.
And so, questions. Existential. *What are*
*you doing here? Where are you coming*
*from? Where are you going after this?*
Best as we could, we answered them. It's

been years now, and still I have questions
to ask the night that let us leave and live
to tell the tale. It's simple, really, what
I want: nothing thrilling; a night that is
as mundane as rain. Three Nigerian-
American boys walk back, late night, from
a Valero with snacks and soda. They cross
the street and stand by a Toyota that belongs
to one of them. They laugh like hyenas until
the night grows jealous of the light in their eyes
and whisks them home and oh, their bodies—
how light, how light they were. And are & are.

# THE WORLD'S LOUDEST SOUND

*Harris County does not have a noise ordinance, as many of the municipalities in our area do. Noise ordinances can specifically target an offense, such as loud music from a vehicle, where if an officer hears it, they may issue a citation.*

—Lieutenant Donald Wine from Harris County Sheriff's Office · 18 May 2016

let's call a group of black
bodies a concert for where

two or three of my people be
there be a song so loud
it'll force

at least one
person to make

at the very least a noise
complaint & of course they will
promise that they didn't

want to do it but had to
you know 'cause there's a baby

sleeping or he'll say sorry
the wife

& i have been
having trouble sleeping lately
you know i tried but just can't

take the noise
anymore you
understand right

and oh just so
you know

a loud noise can
cause damage
to the ears

or neighborhoods
same difference

.  .  .

i read somewhere
that THE LOUDEST
SOUND IN THE WORLD
WOULD KILL YOU
ON THE SPOT

.  .  .

facts: the loudest animal
on earth is the sperm
whale a sheep's got
vibrato in its bleat singing
in vibrato ain't no child's
play ain't something
the untrained got in
they voice one
is from the vocal
cord you could
listen to a sheep
bleating or Eartha

to hear what this
sound like the other
is from the throat for this
listen to the blues in 1883
what i imagine to be
the loudest concert
ever recorded was heard
2223 miles away on a monday
morning in august as sheep
in a camp held a concert
of their own effortlessly showing
off the vibrato in their vocal
cords the loudest concert
sounded like shots from a rifle
from that far away except
all the rifles around had a
long night and have not
yet woken up and so their
throats have no bullets to
spit out for the sky who
with shaky hands can't
hold on to them for long
and so, let's go
and look at the fields how
they do not yield flowers
but instead bullets but i
digress this day the loudest
concert does not ask a rifle
to be an instrument that
ends the song of a body
or two in bleeding, no,
not today, today it is a
monday morning in august
it is the 27th day and 22
23 miles away an entire island
erupts but the sheep don't know

nothing about volcanoes
or the smoke that envelopes
the air after the end of a sad
song so they just carry on
with their bleating

...

i read that
the krakatoa
eruption circled
the earth once
& again & again

& again

& must i tell you
that if we listen
close      enough

we can still hear

the rattle of bones
that once supported
the frame of

more than 36
000 bodies

& some say 40,000
but really who's
counting each bone

a precious metal
melted into an alloy
choker a chorus

so harmonious
we wouldn't have been
able to tell which voice
belonged to whom

...

facts: Effective
January 1, 1808

the importation
of slaves was

outlawed & did
you know that
on those ships

they stacked
bodies on top
of bodies and

this was a beautiful
chord to the ears
of the men who

held the keys
to the chains

that kept
my people
shackled
to the deck

of the ships
that took

them far
away from
the land
where
their
mothers
once
sang
them
to sleep
underneath
a moon-lit sky

& of course, it's so silly
of me but i'm wondering
if slavery was just not
loud enough

before this

that no one bothered
to file a noise complaint

or say something like
this song i don't like it
turn it off all the way
off but no no

everyone slept

just fine through the night
& woke up in the morning
just fine but of course when
we bring up history they say

that's an old song come on

let's play a new song except
there's nothing new about any
of the songs just modified lyrics

but the melody is still
exactly the same


. . .


& yes, the song
of our bodies
still be loud

it is no wonder
they want to
silence it
so bad

# S.W.A.T., ALWAYS

*after Gerald Smith*

Always there'll be / a one room apartment / on the corner of
Wilcrest / & South Dr / or the intersection / of Somewhere &
Anywhere Blvd / Always a family / foreign / an ocean trying
to fit itself inside a cup / Always a people / vast / like the waist-
deep sea of life / they're trying / always trying / to wade
through / Always in the apartment across / a neighbor / you
say good morning or night to / for years without knowing / his
name / or where he's from Always a gas station / with an
attendant / who can claim he knows you / and you wouldn't
dare / deny it / even if he doesn't know your name / Always /
somewhere / someone who knows / your name and yells it out
loud / Always on Bissonnet / a parade you will not / until years
later / know by its true name / Always things we all know / but
don't speak of out loud / Always / somewhere / a hoop Always
a group of boys a patrol car / gon' think is up to / no good
Always some good / folk trying so hard / to kick old / bad
habits Always for the boys / new kicks / Always / too / old
kicks passed down / Always pride and joy either way / Either
way / boys stay fly always / Edge up always on point / heads
always mimicking the sea and its never ceasing waves / Always
somewhere nearby / a mother  screaming / her kids' heads off
because / who know / to straighten us / up  better than our
mothers / and barbers / Always / this place these streets /
where my heart / and feet / find sure footing / Heat or high
water / My voice / is forever rising here / Here / in Houston

## POEM COMPOSED ON THE OCCASION OF THE OPENING OF THE FIRST PAN AFRICAN LIBRARY IN HOUSTON, TX TO COMMEMORATE 400 YEARS OF AFRICAN-AMERICAN HISTORY

Enough has been said about the history of hunger
satiated with the bodies of men, women and children
with ebony skin and ivory teeth, but then, the *White
Lion*. Who was the first to see it, and did she, as she
drew water from a nearby river, leave her pot and run
to the village to warn her kinfolk of its arrival? Was it

through force, or was it because they were enamored
by its enamel coat, that they found themselves, those who
did, inside the stomach of the animal? What did they make
of its rumbling? Did they mistake the percussion of its growl
for an invitation to dance? Here I stand, on the other side
of the past, with questions, but what could I have expected

from the beast, except that it must, as is natural, fill its stomach
like a writer must the white page with words? Here I stand,
asking: In what courtroom will the Atlantic stand in the dock,
one day, as witness, to give an account…? I could stop here,
but it is so natural: this will to continue. Is it not an inheritance?
And is it not right to account for breath? I woke up today—*did I*

*not?*—and did not have to think of the weight of my body
in corn ears, or pounds of tobacco. I'm saying no one traded
my body for smoke. No threshing floor was made ready
for my body to dehusk it of its grains. Soon, I'll be done
with the past and the pressing questions it begs out of me,
but what prayer could my mouth utter now, on new soil,

oceans away from home, except that the earth beneath
my feet open so I may return to it as seed for a tree, which
in turn will be felled to make a shelf to hold, like a mother
would her child, all the books that hold in them the history

of men, women and children with skin and teeth like mine
before the *White Lion* thirsted for their flesh? We had a genesis

before this, did we not? I'm saying a library just might be
the answer to an ancestor's prayer. And look,—won't you
say it is good?—this thing we've made of the freight of the past.

# JUNE 19 IN HISTORY

*I did something good: I made Juneteenth very famous. It's actually an important event, an important time. But nobody had ever heard of it.*

———————————

Today, in Galveston, a woman I love is in a classroom with a group of kids and together, they write poems in the manner of recipes. Here, an hour and thirty minutes' drive from her, I am reading the words of the first Native American to assume the position of the country's Poet Laureate. In the last line of the poem I am reading, we end (by which, I also mean, begin) with the world ending, perhaps, at a kitchen table.

Today, some men run, pigskin in hand, through a field the way a tractor does through acres of wheat and rice.

Today, the prisons are not empty; the cubicles of our workplaces are not.

Today, a rebellion begins.

Today, a battleship is launched; a war is lost & a war is lost.

Today, a riot; a mosque is bombed.

Today, the warlord of a dynasty dies.

Today, a shogun is born.

Today, a poet, a poem.

Today, a bridge collapses and a train slithers into the mouth of a river.

Today, time is collapsed.

Today, all my mother's children are here with her. She wraps her arms around us like a promise kept. I know not what tomorrow has in the pantry, but today, we do not die of hunger.

Today, the village on my tongue dances to the music of the oil in the pan as my brother puts into it what has been cut & crushed to satisfy the god of hunger.

Today, I remember to give thanks—for the sound of running water, that the red that ends up down the sink's drain is only tomato paste.

# A PRAISE SONG FOR THE DAY CHINUA ACHEBE MET JAMES BALDWIN, ENDING IN *PRECIOUS LORD, TAKE MY HAND*

jimmy you were right    to call yourself    a kind of jeremiah    you who spoke
without fear & with    eloquence & clarity    & intelligence like of ancient

african griots & old    testament prophets    your mouth a burning bush
& don't the embers    of your critical intelligence    still brightly burn

long before i met you    i went to rutgers    & met the invisible
man & the darker    brother who sings    america too & the brown
girl who lived in a brown    stone & the one who shed    jones like dead

skin & clothed    himself in blessing    a force of character
but none of them    were like you    two decades after

my country freed    itself from the tight grip    of the colonial
lord (forgive me    there i go again    speaking about his hands)
i meet you    & jimmy i believe you    when you say

109

okonkwo is    your father    so shall we speak

then    of our fathers       & about the miracle of

how they got over & how it will    forever baffle us

have your say        mister baldwin go ahead                                    & we will

make our entire bodies ears for you          do make this day              the day

you speak of white supremacy           & how it's had its day            oh sing

of the day    past & gone    oh sing us through  & out

the night's unlatched jaw    & though tired    weak &

worn we are   we will walk    through the storm

with the undying   embers in your cry

& call to        forever

                 guide our feet

        & keep us    warm

# HERE,

*after Danez Smith, with a line from Ebony Stewart*

Who tryna start shit,
when Harriet Tubman
got eyes everywhere?

And yeah, of course
she strapped. Tell me,
what we need Police for

when we not at war
no more? Here,

every morning we wake up,

we don't gotta worry
about what will end us

before the moon shows
her face. And surely,

something eventually will
pull the cloak over us

and transport us into a new
world, but at least it will not be

the tight grip of The Law.

Tell me, what we need Police
for when even the Police can't
police they self? And ain't that

Lawless? Look, hear
        what I'm not saying.
Hear me.
    I ain't saying

    a world where
        The Law don't exist

gon' be flawless, but
        I woke up

like this—

    like everyone here
        did—with every bee
            in the hive buzzing

us into a new dawn.
    I ain't got no country

but this. Beyoncé say: say
        *Flawless* and just like that,

    everything is
        and that is the only law.
    Here, we
        know no other name

to call ourselves. Here,
        no one can call you & I

        by any name
        our Mamas
        ain't give us.

In the world

we belonged to
before this, they marked us
beasts. But we know
whose image we made in...
...Yeah, we know
the Truth. Sojourner,
before Gage stole her
voice, say to ask you:
am I not, like the rest
of my kinfolk,
a child of God
too?

*...O, who will come and go with me...*
*...Sweet fields arrayed in living green*
*And rivers of Delight.* Here,

when Nina sings
of strange fruit, she not
singing
of our bodies. Nah, she singing
of the "few bad apples" they kept
talking about in the old world, yet refused
to toss out. Now ain't that strange?
Here,

in this new world, we don't need
no trees. We feast

on whatever grows
from the palms of our ancestors. Here
the hands are protected from the oppressors. Here,
we got no dark
clouds to remind us

of what's hanging
over us. Here,

on this bridge
that connects us
to the old world,

Lucille's voice
is a horn, loud.

And so, we march,
everyday,

in celebration.
We remember

the flames, how

the old world turned
ruins, became a field

of bones. And here we are, singing,
unsinged, our mothers here

with us. Here, every morning

we breathe
in the fresh air, we dance

on the ashes

of what remains
of the old world. Here,
[              ]
blows smoke in the face of The Law

and she does not disappear. No,
not here. Not ever.

# A TOAST

*for February & every single month*

Let me attempt what seems impossible.
To carve, like Strazza did a veil, a song of praise
from stone. To the charred teeth of History—black
as the hide of our fathers' belts. To what we can't rinse
out its bloody mouth. To Jimi Hendrix & his *Black
Beauty*. To Esperanza & her bass. To the gravel
and coffee & cream of Nina's voice. To mine,
singing along with her. *To Be Young, Gifted and Black*.
To my sister's & mother's & daughter's hair. To
the coils of smoke snaking through the air above
us. To the roads we have traversed—forked
as the tail of the Saw-wing. To what swallows
and is swallowed. To what we cannot save
from rot. To *my* body, that it is, today, not a burden.
To the palms pricked by the thorn of living.
To the side-eye; to what does not need to be said
with the mouth. To what the horn attempts to say,
because the mouth cannot. To Satchmo's lips. To
the Black Lip Bastard & his Hippy crew. To *Everyone
I'm Rooting For*. To you—named Nameless,
or left unnamed. To the anaphora of breath—
each, like God's little toe, a comma in the sentence
of our lives. To the long winter & how it makes us forget
how Summer thirsts for blood. To Time
and the passing of it. To what is poured out
in memory of those no longer with us. To us; to us.

# Acknowledgements

Many thanks to the editors of the following publications, in which earlier/different versions of individual poems have appeared, or are forthcoming: *The Adroit Journal*, THRILLER NIGHT; *ALL Review*, A TOAST; *Alternating Current Press' Footnote #5*, FOR SAMUEL AJAYI CROWTHER; *Another Chicago Magazine*, CORPUS ALIENUM and IT'S TRUE. I LEFT A *SHITHOLE COUNTRY*; *Barzakh Magazine*, SO, HOW DOES IT FEEL TO BE A CITIZEN? OR, THE DAY AMERICA ASKED ME ABOUT MY MOTHER & I SAID: WHO? I DO NOT KNOW THAT WOMAN!* ; A PRAISE SONG FOR THE DAY CHINUA ACHEBE MET JAMES BALDWIN, ENDING IN "PRECIOUS LORD, TAKE MY HAND" (as THE DAY CHINUA ACHEBE MET JAMES BALDWIN) and MAMA SAY; *Berkeley Poetry Review*, ALIEN REGISTRATION, or the DS-230 is an animal with 2 parts and AN EXAMINATION OF / ON THE MONOLITH (OR, ON BEING JOYFUL & NIGERIAN); *Flypaper Magazine*, A TRANSCRIPT OF AN OVERHEARD CONVERSATION BETWEEN MARGARET WALKER AND YOUNG THUG (as FOR MY PEOPLE: MARGARET WALKER AND YOUNG THUG IN CONVERSATION) and NOTHING GHAZAL (as GHAZAL, MOSTLY IN THE VOICE OF FELA); *the museum of americana*, JUNE 19 IN HISTORY; *Muzzle Magazine*, PRAYER; *New Delta Review*, A LAMENT FOR THE SECOND STANZA OF THE NIGERIAN NATIONAL ANTHEM; *Nimrod Journal*, THE WORLD'S LOUDEST SOUND; *Obsidian: Literature & Arts in the African Diaspora*, FAILED SONNET and SOME DAYS I STAND IN FRONT OF THE MIRROR AND REMIND MYSELF; *Palette Poetry*, AFRICANAMERICAN'T SONNET; *Santa Fe Writers Project*, IN WHICH I INTERVIEW MYSELF AFTER WATCHING *BLACK PANTHER*; *Solstice Literary Magazine*, I

WALK INTO EVERY ROOM AND DO NOT NEED TO YELL WHERE THE NIGERIANS AT; *Sonora Review*, UPON COMING ACROSS THE MIGRATORY BIRD TREATY ACT OF 1918; *The Texas Review*, IN WHICH I ERASE [AND ADD TO THE] N-652, MY NATURALIZATION INTERVIEW RESULTS; *Third Coast*, MY MOTHER SAYS I SPEAK IN MY MOTHER TONGUE; *Verity La*, ON DIASPORA: A SHORT ESSAY; *Write About Now*, THE ONE IN WHICH MY FATHER REMINDS ME YET AGAIN OF THE GROUND, OR MY FATHER IS A PEACOCK? AN EAGLE? IDK. (as MY FATHER IS A PEACOCK? AN EAGLE? IDK.)

Additionally, HERE, is included for publication in Cambridge Writers' Workshop's forthcoming anthology, *Disobedient Futures*; S.W.A.T., ALWAYS was featured in *By Way of, Houston*, a 2021 docuseries by Loyce Gayo and was part of Deborah "D.E.E.P." Mouton's *The Houston Emerge Project* (2019); ALTERNATIVE and GENESIS (published as SORRY, LET US START AT BIRTH, THE BEGINNING) were included in the anthology, *CONTRA: Texas Poets Speak Out* (FlowerSong Press, 2020) which was edited by Rooster Martinez and Chibbi Orduña; a selection of poems from this manuscript was chosen by Selah Saterstrom as the winner of *New Delta Review*'s 8th Annual Chapbook Contest and was published as *African, American* in 2019; Also in 2019, FOR SAMUEL AJAYI CROWTHER was a finalist for *Alternative Current Press'* Charter Oak Award for Best Historical, and a chapbook version of this manuscript was selected as the Center for Book Arts 2019 Chapbook Contest Runner Up; LORD      TEACH MY THROAT was printed as a limited edition broadside; in 2018, FOR MY PEOPLE: MARGARET WALKER AND YOUNG THUG IN CONVERSATION was selected by Hanif Abdurraqib as the winner of *Flypaper Magazine*'s Music Contest, and THE WORLD'S LOUDEST SOUND was selected as a finalist for *Nimrod Journal*'s The

Pablo Neruda Prize in Poetry, which was judged by Patricia Smith. ALIEN REGISTRATION, or the DS-230 is an animal with 2 parts & AN EXAMINATION OF / ON THE MONOLITH (OR, ON BEING JOYFUL & NIGERIAN) were also published in the *Berkeley Poetry Review*'s chapbook, *Midterm 2: Counting, and Recounting* in 2018. ALIEN REGISTRATION, or the DS-230 is an animal with 2 parts was also included in Reyes Ramirez's online exhibition, *The Houston Artist Speaks Through Grids.*

My gratitude and debts are equally immense. Thank you, foremost & forever, to my immediate family.

This book would not exist without the works and influences of Patricia Smith, Danez Smith, Hanif Abdurraqib, Solmaz Sharif, Layli Long Soldier, Philip Metres, Marwa Helal, Terrance Hayes, Joshua Bennett, Safia Elhillo, Pages Matam, Loyce Gayo, Mwende "FreeQuency" Katwiwa, Ariana Brown, Ebony Stewart, Deborah "D.E.E.P." Mouton, Natasha Carrizosa, the Black Arts Movement (most especially Amiri Baraka, James Baldwin, Sonia Sanchez & June Jordan) and so many, many, many others. If anything in here sounds like not-me, I most likely stole it from them.

Thank you. Thank you. Thank you.

To MacDowell, for gifting me the space & time to dream up (and actualize) the beginning of this.

To my Houston writing communities. Especially Write About Now, Houston VIP Slam, and Tintero Projects. Thank you for sharpening my voice.

Thank you, Lupe Mendez. Thank you, Jasminne Mendez. Can I ever repay you both!?

To *New Delta Review* (especially Elizabeth Kolenda and Laura Theobald) for ushering *African, American* into the world. Thank you, Selah, for seeing something in it.

To FlowerSong Press/Edward Vidaurre for publishing this expanded version of what started as a chapbook.

I'm so grateful for the countless conversations I've had that have shaped this manuscript and the ongoing project it is a part of. Most notably with Omer Ahmed, Jeremy Eugene, and George Abraham.

Special thanks to Usman Hameedi, Yaw Kyeremateng, Lynn Lane, Joshua Nguyen, Arielle Cottingham, and Aris Kian for your generosity in the final stages of putting together this book you now hold in your hands, dear reader; if you find any subpar poem in these pages, it is because I didn't listen when they told me to toss it.

And dear reader, thank you!

# Notes

In order of appearance, the book's epigraphs are from Mwende "FreeQuency" Katwiwa's *Becoming//Black*, the liner note for *CULTURAL EXCHANGE* (the first section of Langston Hughes' *Ask Your Mama: 12 Moods for Jazz*), W. E. B. Du Bois' essay, *Criteria of Negro Art* and Ariana Brown's *At the End of the Borderlands*—from the collection, *We Are Owed*.

**UPON COMING ACROSS THE MIGRATORY BIRD TREATY ACT OF 1918**'s epigraph is from a video on National Geographic's YouTube channel (*Masters of Migration | National Geographic*) published on September 16, 2009. The concept for Section II was inspired by Linette Reeman's repeated use of concept in *After My History Class Debates Whether the Snake in the Garden of Eden Is Male or Female*. The epigraphs in Section III are from Ulrich B. Phillips' *American Negro Slavery: A Survey of the Supply, Employment, and Control of Negro Labor, as Determined by the Plantation Regime. (1918).* The end note (italicized) is from *What Is The Migratory Bird Treaty Act?* via allaboutbirds.org.

**CORPUS ALIENUM**, translated from Latin, means a foreign body. The source of the poem's litany of objects is the British 'shockumentary' series *101 Things Removed from the Human Body* and *101 More Things Removed from the Human Body*.

The prose excerpts in **PORTRAIT OF MY FATHER WITH PLINY'S BIRDS: A NATURAL HISTORY** is from a January 14, 1911 letter addressed to The Editor of *The Spectator* (found here: http:// archive.spectator.co.uk /article/14th-january-1911/16/a-bird-of-nigeria) while the found poems between the excerpts are taken from Pliny the

Elder's *The Natural History*. More specifically, from the Raven, Crow, Phoenix, and Ostrich chapters of *Book X. The Natural History of Birds*.

The epigraph for **THE ONE IN WHICH MY FATHER REMINDS ME YET AGAIN OF THE GROUND, OR MY FATHER IS A PEACOCK? AN EAGLE? IDK.** is from *A History of the Airplane* via wright-brothers.org

**FAILED SONNET** was prompted by a news article written by Fikayo Olowolagba (published in *Daily Post Nigeria* on June 27, 2018) and is for Obioma Odum.

In **PRAYER**, "no one turns over the earth when a black girl goes missing" is from Ebony Stewart's "White Men Say Weird Things To Me."

In **MY MOTHER SAYS I SPEAK IN MY MOTHER TONGUE**, the question—italicized and bolded—is taken from Question 3 of the West African Examinations Council (WAEC) *Yoruba Paper 2*, May/June 2010. The beginning of the response to the question: "of course, this is about language / & who / & what the language holds / in place..." is a variation of the opening line of Danez Smith's "my nig."

**S.M., THE YOUNG AFRICAN PAINTER RESPONDS** is in conversation with (and quotes from) Phillis Wheatley's "To S. M., a Young African Painter, on Seeing His Works."

**SORRY I AM NOT HIM I AM THE OTHER AFRICAN POET** is for the Ghanaian poet, Yaw Kyeremateng.

**PALINODE** gestures to Toni Morrison's Nobel Lecture.

Bolaji Badejo, whom **XENOMORPH XX121** is written for/addressed to, starred as the titular creature of the 1979 film Alien.

**HOW CAN I GIVE A NAME TO WHAT I AM** owes its title and a portion of its opening line to the philosopher Martin Heidegger. In "A Dialogue on Language," Heidegger, in a fictional reconstruction of a conversation between him and Professor Tomio Tezuka, asks: "How is one to give a name to what he is still searching for?" Another translation renders the question as: "How can I give a name to what I'm still searching for?" The poem alludes to Amiri Baraka's "Black Art" ("Fuck poems / And they are useful..." and is, additionally, indebted to/in conversation with Claude McKay's "If We Must Die," César Vallejo's "Black Stone on a White" Stone and Donald Justice's "Variation On A Text by Vallejo."

**NOTHING GHAZAL** contains interpolated lyrics from songs by Fela Kuti. The epigraph is from Loyce Gayo's "Politics at God's Funeral."

The first question & answer (italicized) in **IN WHICH I INTERVIEW MYSELF AFTER WATCHING *BLACK PANTHER*** reference & quotes Ryan Coogler from Tre'vell Anderson's write-up: "Why *Black Panther* is Ryan Coogler's most personal film to date." *Los Angeles Times*. 15 Feb. 2018. Accessed 20 Feb. 2018. "Are you done?" & "don't scare me like that, colonizer" are quotes from *Black Panther*.

In **A TRANSCRIPT OF AN OVERHEARD CONVERSATION BETWEEN MARGARET WALKER AND YOUNG THUG,** "…a poet spoke / of the god of trying…" references Zachary Caballero's "How a Mango Makes a Man, Again."

**AFRICANAMERICAN'T SONNET** references this line—"Love means you breathe in two countries"—from Naomi Shihab Nye's "Two Countries." I like to think of it as a less impressive, wannabe, cousin of Marwa Helal's "poem to be read from right to left."

**THRILLER NIGHT** is for Charles Ademolu and James Ekeke who walked with me that night.

The *White Lion* mentioned in **POEM COMPOSED ON THE OCCASION OF THE OPENING OF THE FIRST PAN AFRICAN LIBRARY IN HOUSTON, TX TO COMMEMORATE 400 YEARS OF AFRICAN-AMERICAN HISTORY** was the name of the ship that brought the first documented Africans to Virginia (at, what was then, Point Comfort) in late August, 1619. The poem is dedicated to the SAiD Pan African Library.

**JUNE 19 IN HISTORY** references Joy Harjo and her poem, "Perhaps the World Ends Here."

**A PRAISE SONG FOR THE DAY CHINUA ACHEBE MET JAMES BALDWIN** primarily uses Chinua Achebe's account in "The Day I Finally Met Baldwin" as source text. The opening line "…you were right to call yourself a kind of Jeremiah" is from Baldwin's essay, "The American Dream and